Incredible
Amphibians

John Townsend

Raintree

www.raintreepublishers.co.uk

Visit our website to find out more information about **Raintree** books.

To order:
☎ Phone 44 (0) 1865 888113
▤ Send a fax to 44 (0) 1865 314091
▢ Visit the Raintree Bookshop at **www.raintreepublishers.co.uk** to browse our catalogue and order online.

First published in Great Britain by Raintree, Halley Court, Jordan Hill, Oxford OX2 8EJ, part of Harcourt Education. Raintree is a registered trademark of Harcourt Education Ltd.

Editorial: Charlotte Guillain and Diyan Leake
Design: Michelle Lisseter and Kamae Design
Picture Research: Maria Joannou
Production: Jonathan Smith

Originated by Ambassador
Printed and bound in Hong Kong, China by South China Printing Company

ISBN 1 844 43327 7
08 07 06 05 04
10 9 8 7 6 5 4 3 2 1

British Library Cataloguing in Publication Data
Townsend, John
Incredible Amphibians. – (Incredible Creatures)
597.8
A full catalogue record for this book is available from the British Library.

Acknowledgements
The publisher would like to thank the following for permission to reproduce photographs: Bryan & Cherry Alexander p. 40 left; Corbis pp. 20 (Lynda Richardson), 24 right (David A. Northcott), 42–3 (Phil Schermeister), 48 bottom (Martin B. Withers/Frank Lane Picture Agency), 51 (Fadek Timothy); Digital Vision pp. 5 bottom, 32; FLPA pp. 6 right (John Tinning), 7 (Michael Clark), 8 right (Yossi Eshbol), 12 right (Albert Visage), 12 left (Roger Wilmshurst), 13 (Minden Pictures), 16 (Alwyn J. Roberts), 16–17 (Michael Clark), 18 bottom (Tony Hamblin), 22 right (David Hosking), 24 left (Richard Brooks), 26 right (Silvestris), 27 (G. Marcoaldi/Panda Photos), 28 (Alwyn J. Roberts), 28–9 (Martin B. Withers), 30 left (B. Borrell), 31, 33 (Minden Pictures), 40 right (Chris Mattison), 47 (B. S. Turner); Getty Images p. 10 right; Naturepl pp. 14 (Morley Read), 39 (Jose B. Ruiz), 46 (Dietmar Nill); NHPA pp. 4, 4–5 (Stephen Dalton), 5 top (Stephen Dalton), 5 middle (Stephen Dalton), 6 left (Stephen Dalton), 8 left (Rod Planck), 9 (National Geographic), 10 left (Stephen Dalton), 11 (John Shaw), 14–15 (Daniel Heuclin), 15 (Jany Sauvanet), 18 top (Stephen Dalton), 19 (G. I. Bernard), 20–1 (Stephen Dalton), 21 (Stephen Dalton), 22 left (Daniel Heuclin), 26 left (Daniel Heuclin), 29 (Stephen Dalton), 30 right (Ant Photo Library), 34–5 (Robert Erwin), 36 (Ant Photo Library), 36–7 (Daniel Heuclin), 37 (Ant Photo Library), 38 bottom (Stephen Dalton), 38 top (Ant Photo Library), 41 (Karl Switak), 43 (Stephen Dalton), 44 (Ralph & Daphne Keller), 44–5 (Stephen Dalton), 48 top (Bill Coster), 49 (Ant Photo Library), 50 (Stephen Dalton); Oxford Scientific Films pp. 17 (David M. Dennis), 23 (Dess & Jen Bartlett/FAL), 32–3 (Nick Gordon), 34 (Alan & Sandy Carey), 42; Photodisc p. 25; Photofusion pp. 50–1 (David Preston); Science Photo Library 45 (Dr Morley Read)

Cover photograph of a green frog reproduced with permission of Science Photo Library (David N. Davis)

The publishers would like to thank Jon Pearce for his assistance in the preparation of this book.

Every effort has been made to contact copyright holders of any material reproduced in this book. Any omissions will be rectified in subsequent printings if notice is given to the publishers.

The paper used to print this book comes from sustainable resources.

Contents

Any words appearing in the text in bold, **like this**, are explained in the Glossary. You can also look out for them in the 'Wild words' bank at the bottom of each page.

The world of amphibians

Would you believe it?

- One of the smallest frogs was discovered in Cuba in 1997. It is only 1 centimetre long and could sit on your fingernail.

- The largest amphibian is the Chinese giant salamander. It grows up to 1.8 metres long and weighs over 30 kilograms. One of those would sit on your whole body if it sat on you!

Amphibians live two lives. They start off as a blob of jelly in water. Small black dots grow inside the jelly and then hatch. These tiny creatures swim under water and breathe through **gills**. Then something amazing happens. They grow legs, climb out of the water and crawl over the mud. They can live on dry land or in water.

Amphibians are like **reptiles** such as snakes because they are cold-blooded. That means they do not make their own body heat but depend on the air or water around them to control their temperature. They only become active when they are warm.

Yet amphibians are unlike reptiles because they do not have **scales**. In fact, they have smooth, damp, hairless skin that lets water through.

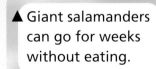
▲ Giant salamanders can go for weeks without eating.

Wild words   **gills**   flaps that some animals have to breathe under water
reptile   cold-blooded animal with scales, such as a snake or lizard

Three groups

There are more than 4000 **species** of amphibian. The biggest group is the frog and toad family. There are more than 3500 species of frog and toad.

Then there are about 360 types of salamander. This group includes newts. They all have long, thin bodies with tails. Some salamanders live entirely on land, but others never leave the water. Others spend some time in the water and some time on land.

The third group of amphibians are the **caecilians**. They have no legs and look like large worms. Most live under ground and spend their time in the soil, but a few live in water.

Find out later...

What is an axolotl?

How can a toad live inside a solid rock?

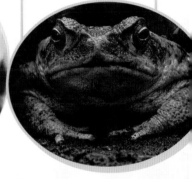

How can a frog kill you?

Fast facts

'Amphibian' comes from two ancient Greek words. Amphi means 'both'. Bios means 'life'. Put them together and they describe the two lives of amphibians.

▲ Like all frogs, the common frog has very powerful back legs.

scales small bony plates that protect the skin – as on fish and reptiles
species type of animal or plant

Meet the family

You might not believe this...

A single frog can lay as many as 20,000 eggs. But sometimes, strange things can happen to those eggs. If a **whirlwind** scoops up water along the banks of lakes, eggs and **tadpoles** can be sucked up into the air. Later it can rain tadpoles and frogs!

The amphibian family is one of the oldest on Earth. Amphibians may have been around for up to 400 million years. Scientists think **ancient** amphibians dragged themselves out of swamps and slowly began to **evolve**. Over millions of years their bodies changed to suit life on land. **Fossils** show that the earliest known frog appeared about 190 million years ago.

A frog's back legs became longer and stronger than its front legs. This helped it jump to move across land and to escape danger. Frogs are now the most widespread amphibians of all. They are found just about everywhere except for on a few islands, at the North and South poles or in the driest deserts.

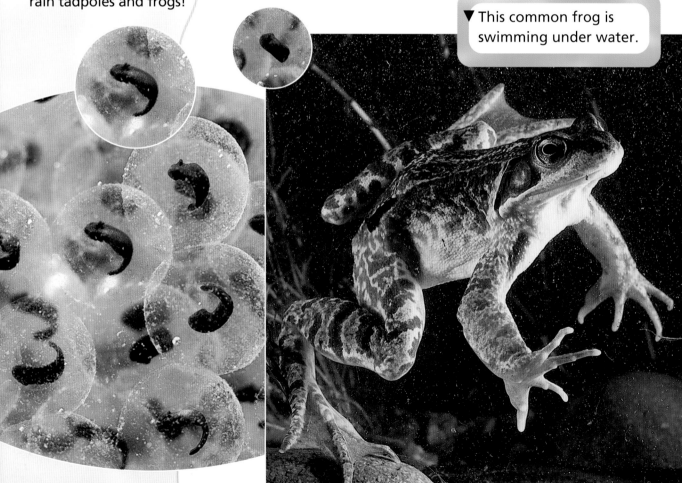

▼ This common frog is swimming under water.

Wild words   **drought**   long period with no rain and a shortage of water
evolve   develop and change over time

Frogs and toads

Frogs have several special features:

- two bulging eyes on the sides of their head
- strong, long, webbed back feet that are adapted for leaping and swimming. They have no tail.
- smooth skin that is often slimy. The slime that oozes from a frog's skin stops it from drying out and helps to protect it from **predators** so it can slip away. The slime also helps to draw **oxygen** in through the frog's skin.

During long periods of heat, severe cold or **drought**, many frogs tend to 'close down'. They **hibernate** until conditions improve. Most frogs like damp areas, yet some can cope with quite dry places. Most frogs lay eggs in clusters but toads lay theirs in strings.

Flying frogs

- In 1954, thousands of young frogs fell like snow in the West Midlands of England.

- In 1882 in Dubuque, Iowa, USA, a hailstorm was a bit odd. One hailstone had two frogs inside. When the ice melted, there sat two live frogs!

▼ Common frogs on the march!

Turn to page 40 to find out if frogs can be frozen and still live.

---

hibernate 'close down' the body and rest when it is too cold or dry
oxygen one of the gases in air and water that all living things need

When is a toad not a toad?

When it is a lizard! The horned toad is not a type of frog at all. It is a lizard that lives in the deserts of North America. This small **reptile** can squirt blood from its eyes to startle an attacker.

Toads

About 400 types of frog are called toads. They all belong to the family Bufonidae.

Toads tend to stay on land more than other frogs. They also look different because they have:

- stubby bodies with short back legs for walking instead of hopping
- bumpy and dry skin. They often live in drier places.
- **glands** behind the eyes that can ooze poison. This is often just a weak slimy poison but enough to make a cat or a dog froth at the mouth if it catches a toad. Only a few toads make poison strong enough to harm pets or humans.

▼ The horned toad's real name is the Texas horned lizard.

► A green toad looks as if it has warts, but it is just bumpy skin.

gland   part of the body that makes hormones and other substances

Toxic toads

A toad's skin tends to be bumpy because of the poisons that come from its glands. These bumps are not warts and despite old tales, toads do not give you warts.

One toad in particular makes a very strong poison. This **species** was brought to Australia from South America and it is now a real problem.

MARCH OF THE TOXIC TOADS

2001

An army of **toxic** toads is on the march across northern Australia. The deadly amphibians are spreading at a rate of about 96 kilometres (60 miles) a year. When threatened, the toads ooze poison that can kill people if they dare to swallow it. Already many snakes, lizards, turtles and birds have died from biting the toads. Any animal that gets a dose of the toads' poison can die within 15 minutes. Even crocodiles leave them alone.

Not many people know this

What do you call a group of frogs? What do you call a group of toads?

Answer: A *chorus* (or sometimes an *army*) of frogs and a *knot* of toads.

⋗ ⋗ ⋗ ⋗ ⋗ ⋗ ⋗ ⋗

Find out what these toads are and why they are also in the USA – on page 36.

◀ One frog and a few toads fight for space in a pond.

toxic   poisonous

Axolotl

The axolotl ('acks-o-lot-ol', shown below) is an unusual salamander from Mexico. Some axolotls grow into full adults and live on land. Others stay in water and do not develop lungs. Even though they stay as 'big babies', they develop in other ways and are able to breed.

Salamanders

Many salamanders look like lizards with smooth skins. There are many different sorts and sizes, with some salamanders being able to live in and out of water. Some are called 'lungless' and look like eels with legs. Some live in dark caves and they are blind.

Hellbenders

There are three **species** of giant salamander that have a large, heavy body and a short tail. One of these is the hellbender that lives in the USA. The largest hellbender ever recorded was just over 72 centimetres long. Its close relative in Japan and China can reach almost 2 metres long. Hellbenders have large **limbs** and feet with five toes. They are very slimy and difficult to handle. Hellbenders have many tiny teeth but they do not often try to bite humans.

▲ Hellbenders are also called devil dogs. They might seem scary but they are harmless.

limb   moving part that sticks out from a body like an arm or leg
spiny   having lots of spines and spikes

Quick facts on salamanders

- Some salamanders are called newts. **Spiny** salamanders like the Chinese spiny newt have sharp ribs that poke out of their skin. This stops many **predators** from taking a bite.
- Lungless salamanders have to take in **oxygen** through their skin and mouth lining. This means they must always stay damp. If they dry out, the oxygen cannot get into their body. Lungless salamanders such as the red, dusky and slimy salamanders live in damp areas of North and South America.
- An old story tells that salamanders like fire. This is probably because they often hide in old logs. When these logs were thrown onto fires, the salamanders would run out. People thought they lived inside the flames!

Old age

In zoos and as pets, some amphibians can live for many years. Some salamanders have **survived** for 20 to 25 years, and a few have lived for more than 50 years.

▼ The long-tailed salamander lives among rocks, logs and plants in forests in North America.

survive   to stay alive despite danger and difficulties

Colourful species

The great crested newt (shown below) is also called the warty newt. It has a rough and bumpy skin. It also has a crest along its back. In the UK it is an **endangered** species. That means it is against the law to harm them in any way.

Newts

Newts are the smaller, lizard-like salamanders less than 17 centimetres long that live mostly in water. Nearly all newts live in the northern half of the world. They do not live in the wild in Australia or in many other southern countries at all. In fact, the only natural Australian amphibians are frogs.

Like many salamanders, newts have four short legs and a long, strong tail. The tail is important for balancing when they walk on land. Yet its main use is to **propel** newts through water when they swim.

Newts tend to keep well hidden. They hide in cool, damp places in the day and they come out at night to feed on snails and insects. Because of this, we do not see them often.

▶ Marbled newts are found in Spain, Portugal and parts of France.

endangered   at risk of disappearing forever
propel   drive along and push forward

Legs and tails

There are at least 300 salamander **species**. About 60 of these are different sorts of newts. Many newts have long flaps of skin on the top and bottom of their tail. This helps them swim with speed.

Some newts can do strange things with their tails. If something grabs them, newts can **shed** their tails. Some lizards can do this, too. After a while they just grow a new one. But that is not all. If a newt loses a leg, it does not matter. After a few months a new one grows. No one really knows how this happens. It seems to have something to do with changes in the blood. Cells start dividing to heal the injury. The newt just gets on with its life!

American newt

The young eastern newt of North America is red with spots on its back. The young live on land close to water for 2 or 3 years before they become adults and return to live in water. They tend to be active after dark.

▲ This eastern newt will turn green or brown when it becomes an adult.

shed   get rid of or lose

Mystery amphibians

Caecilians are found in swampy places in most tropical parts of the world. They are hardly ever seen because they are always wriggling in mud or burrowing. They eat small **invertebrates** such as termites and earthworms. There are no known caecilians in Europe, North America, Australia or Antarctica.

▼ A caecilian's skin has folds and it bends itself around easily.

Caecilians

Not a lot is known about these amphibians, as they are not often seen. **Caecilians** look like burrowing snakes or worms. They range in size from a few centimetres to 1.5 metres. Caecilians have no **limbs** at all. They burrow in the soil using their strong skulls as **battering rams** and swim by moving their **muscular** bodies back and forth like eels.

There are about 160 **species** and they all live in tropical forests of South America and Africa. Their colour varies from blackish blue to pink or orange. Some have spots or stripes. Their tiny eyes are covered by skin and often by bone. Many are blind as they spend all of their time under ground.

battering ram   heavy rod used to knock down walls and doors
captivity   a cage or tank – as in a zoo

Slippery customers

Caecilians are sometimes called rubber eels or black eels. If you handle one, it is like a smooth, rubbery tube and it often ties itself in knots. If caecilians are put in a tank, they will tie themselves to anything they can find. They will wriggle round each other, any slow-moving fish or a person's fingers.

In **captivity**, caecilians like to burrow into gravel but they come up for air several times a day. As they cannot see well, if at all, caecilians have to rely on other senses to find food. They have two small feelers between their eyes and nose. These help them find insects and worms to eat.

No legs

The name 'caecilian' comes from a word that means 'blind'. Many species cannot see at all. Another name for these amphibians is 'apod', which means 'no limbs'. These animals are suited to life in mud, whether on land or under water. Caecilians are far safer when buried, as they have many **predators** above ground.

◄ In its dark, muddy world, a caecilian does not need its eyes.

invertebrate   animal without a backbone
muscular   having strong muscles

Amazing bodies

Amphibians' bodies are amazing. They completely change as they grow, their skin can do strange things and the way some of them breathe is very unusual.

Air and water

All animals need **oxygen** to live. That oxygen has to get into the blood and round their bodies. So how do animals get that oxygen from the surrounding air or water? And how do they get rid of all the **carbon dioxide** from their blood? It all seems very simple:

- animals that live in water breathe with **gills**. That is why all fish have gills.
- animals that live on land breathe with lungs. That is why all **mammals**, **reptiles** and birds have lungs.

But what about animals that go to and from water and land? Simple – they have both... sometimes!

Growing up

Frogs have gills only when they are tadpoles, as shown below. As a young frog grows, its gills are **absorbed** into its body and the lungs take over for breathing air.

> > > > > > > > > > > >
Find out more about **tadpoles** like these, and tiny amphibians on page 29.

absorb   take in something or soak it up
carbon dioxide   gas that animals breathe out

Breath of life

When amphibians hatch they are just like little fish. That is because they swim under water and breathe through gills. Gills are slits in the sides of their head. Young amphibians suck water in through their mouths and pass it out through their gills. The gills take oxygen from the water and pass it into blood vessels. The tiny amphibians now have oxygen-rich blood pumping through their body. They can swim about and get rid of the carbon dioxide they do not need – also through their gills.

If there are too many young amphibians in a small puddle of water, they will soon use up all the oxygen and die. They need to live in clean water with plants that make oxygen.

The mudpuppy

Unlike most other salamanders, the mudpuppy of the USA (below) keeps its gills when it grows up. That is because its lungs are not well developed and it stays in muddy ponds. If the oxygen level falls, the mudpuppy takes a gulp of air into its lungs from the surface. Its gills look like red feathers at the sides of its head.

◀ These tadpoles will be using their gills to breathe until they start living on land as frogs

mammal   warm-blooded animal that has hair and feeds its young on milk

17

Back-up system

A growing amphibian has the best of both worlds. It can breathe with both gills and lungs. That means it can swim under water for long periods without regular trips to the surface to gulp air.

Living on land

So most amphibians change their **gills** for lungs as they grow up. Then they can breathe air as they walk on land. But there is more to it than that. How do lungless salamanders breathe?

Adult amphibians have another way of getting **oxygen** into their bodies. They can breathe and 'drink' through their skin. This includes through the lining of the mouth and throat.

Amphibian skin is not waterproof like ours. It lets in moisture and oxygen through tiny blood vessels. Lungless salamanders get all of their oxygen this way.

▼ As water can soak through an amphibian's special skin, most do not drink. Like this common frog, they take in as much water as they need through their skin.

dew   water droplets that form on plants during cool nights
nourishment   food that supplies important nutrients to the body

Skin

Amphibian skin has **glands** that make slime to protect the skin from drying out. The slime also helps to draw in oxygen. Even with slimy skin, most frogs need to stay near water. Toads have tougher skin that does not dry out as fast, so they can live further from water than most frogs.

As well as jumping in water, frogs and toads can get moisture from **dew**, or they can burrow under ground into moist soil. Some toads get over half the water they need through a baggy patch on their **pelvis**. They press it against moist surfaces to **absorb** water into their body.

Frogs **shed** their skin to keep it healthy. Some frogs shed their skin weekly, others as often as every day.

Old skin

Frogs take a while to shed their old skin. They have to wriggle about to get out of it. Once the frog pulls the skin off over its head, like a slimy vest, guess what? The frog eats it! It cannot let good **nourishment** go to waste.

▼ This frog is swallowing its skin before hopping off into the night.

FAST FACTS

Many frogs and toads live for 5 or 10 years. Some can live for more than 30 years.

pelvis   area of bone between the hips

Feeding

Supper time

Amphibians have a special organ in the roof of their mouth for finding food. It is called the Jacobson's organ. This is richly supplied with **nerves** and helps to sense chemicals and different scents in the air. Messages go to the brain to work out if prey is near.

Nearly all adult amphibians are **carnivores**, so they have to hunt for their food. Their **prey** is mainly insects, spiders, worms, small **reptiles** and smaller amphibians. Amphibians rely on their good hearing to find food. Some can sense **vibrations** from likely prey. Often it is a case of just sitting and waiting for something to come along. Amphibians' eyes tend to stick out so they can keep a watch in all directions.

Caecilians rely on their feelers and approach their prey slowly before grabbing it with their sharp teeth. Salamanders that feed in water suck their prey into their mouths. On land, some salamanders flick out their sticky tongues to catch insects.

▲ This red spotted newt is eating an earthworm.

carnivore   meat-eater
nerves   fibres that carry messages between the brain and the rest of the body

Frog food

Frogs can hear and hop very well so any fly that lands nearby has to watch out. Did you know that frogs can jump 20 times their own length using those strong legs of theirs? That would be like you jumping 30 metres straight out of your chair! Some frogs have even hopped over 10 metres in one jump.

Frogs with long tongues use the 'see it, snap it' way of feeding. In a fraction of a second, their tongue unrolls like an upside-down party whistle. With a quick flick, their tongue sticks to any bug, snaps it up and it is gone in a flash! Their aim is always excellent.

Sticky frog

The red-eyed tree frog (shown above) lives in the rainforests of South and Central America. It spends most of its time climbing trees where there are juicy insects. This frog is sticky at both ends. Sticky pads on its toes grip onto leaves and branches. Then its sticky tongue slurps the food.

◄ With one quick leap, a frog can even catch insects in mid-air.

prey   animal that is killed and eaten by other animals
vibration   quivering movement or fast trembling

Big appetites

Toads prefer to eat only moving prey. It is thought that a single toad may catch and eat as many as 10,000 insects in one summer. Unlike frogs, most toads have short tongues and they just snap at their food with their mouth. They often **stalk** their prey before they pounce.

Eating and digesting

Frogs have teeth but toads do not. However, frogs' small teeth are only in their top jaw. They cannot bite very well so frogs depend on their tongues for eating. Fine hairs in their throat sweep food particles down to the stomach. There, the **glands** and juices can get to work to break down the **prey**. Sometimes swallowed insects might still be alive! Slowly the **nutrients** are **absorbed** into the frogs' blood.

When a frog swallows a meal, it has to use as much force as it can to get the food down its throat. Its bulgy eyeballs close and go down into its head. This helps to push the meal right down to its stomach.

▼ An African bullfrog will eat just about anything it can get into its mouth.

nutrients   important substances found in food and needed by the body
stalk   hunt down by following and creeping up on a victim

Horned frogs

Horned frogs are large, flat and very colourful. The horns are really folds of skin just over their eyes. They live in South America and **hibernate** if it gets too dry. They can wait for rain like this for up to 6 months. Horned frogs eat large insects and small **vertebrates** such as lizards, mice and other frogs. They sit and wait for food to come near before they attack. These frogs are sometimes called 'mouths on legs' because the mouth seems to take up the whole of their head. They will eat any animal they can get in their huge mouth – which might just happen to be a smaller horned frog.

Bad taste

Some frogs do not have to worry about what they eat. If they swallow something that is poisonous or bad for them, they just throw up everything in their entire stomach. They wipe the unpleasant food away with their legs and eat the rest again. Don't try this at home!

▼ This female horned frog is swallowing a mouse whole.

vertebrate   animal with a backbone

Breeding

'I'm here!'

Frogs and toads use their keen hearing to **communicate** with one another. Using a voice box and a large vocal sac attached to the throat, they make croaks to call a mate or to tell a rival to 'clear off'.

▼ These red-spotted newts are on their way to their breeding pond to mate.

Amphibians do not mix with each other. Unlike some **mammals** and birds that live in groups or pair up for life, amphibians keep themselves to themselves. The only time they meet up is to breed. Then they go off on their own again. They usually leave their young to get on with life on their own.

Meeting up

Once a year amphibians have to find a mate. They use all sorts of ways to announce that they are ready and waiting.

Little is known about how caecilians meet, but many frogs and salamanders use all kinds of tricks to attract a mate. Noises, movements and showing off colours or pouches signal that a male and female would like to meet.

communicate   make contact and understand another's signals
dewlap   loose flap of skin at the throat

Springtime

In the spring, amphibians are on the move. They head towards their breeding ponds in **swarms**. This is when they are in greatest danger from **predators** or from traffic on roads and railways.

Scientists have found that newts always return to the same breeding pond each spring. In Washington State in the USA, many newts were taken over 1.6 kilometres (1 mile) from their home pond. Each newt found its way back. Masses of males swarmed over each female, making a wriggling pile of newts.

Noisy frogs

Frogs also gather in huge numbers for breeding. Male frogs rely on their calls. Some croak or click or whistle to attract females and to keep other males away. It all gets very noisy.

Showing off

A male frog calls to a mate by squeezing his lungs – with his nostrils and mouth shut. Air flows over his vocal chords and into his vocal sac. This blows it up like a bubble gum balloon. His croak fills the night and the female cannot resist.

▼ These common frogs are meeting up to breed.

◄ The real name for the flap of skin under a frog's mouth is a **dewlap**.

Movers and shakers

Newts and salamanders do not have voices like frogs and toads. They attract each other by showing off some fancy swimming moves. After a kind of underwater dance together, the pair is ready to mate.

Mating

Like **reptiles** and insects, amphibian females lay many eggs at a time. But the male nearly always **fertilizes** the eggs outside the female's body. A pair of frogs will often lock together, with the male clinging to the female's back. As she lays her hundreds of eggs in the water, he releases **sperm**. The **frogspawn** is left to hatch in the water.

Underwater embrace

Newts often cling to each other for hours under water. Then the male leaves small packets of jelly topped with sperm on the riverbed. The female collects this and stores it inside her until she lays her eggs. The eggs are fertilized as she lays them one at a time on plants under the water.

▼ These mating frogs are surrounded by frogspawn.

▲ The male Californian newt rubs his chin on the back of the female's head.

embryo   tiny group of growing cells formed from a fertilized egg
fertilize   when a sperm joins an egg to form a new individual

Eggs in jelly

Amphibian eggs do not have a waterproof shell to protect them. They are not like bird or reptile eggs. Instead, a clear jelly surrounds each egg. A tiny **embryo** begins to grow inside. The eggs need to be in water or in a damp place. Otherwise the embryo will dry out and die. Many amphibians lay their eggs directly in water, but some frogs and salamanders lay their eggs on land. Nearly all caecilians lay eggs in damp places such as **leaf litter**, burrows or wet cracks in the ground under logs or rocks.

Amphibians lay masses of eggs. They have to because so many of them never survive. The lucky ones that manage to hatch still face many dangers. Maybe only 1 egg in every 200 ever grows up. Predators are always waiting to snap up eggs and young amphibians. Sudden storms can also sweep away the eggs. Mothers lay their eggs in still water but heavy rain can soon wash both eggs and young away.

Perfect timing

The female salamander decides when she wants to have her young. The male deposits some jelly beside her, which contains the sperm. When she feels ready, the female draws the jelly from the riverbed into herself. This will fertilize her eggs when she releases them into the water.

▼ For a while these salamander embryos are safe in their eggs under water.

All change

Amphibians produce the most amazing young. That is because they are nothing like their parents and they can survive only under water. They have to go through a huge change to become an adult. This big change is called **metamorphosis**.

Hatching

Newt **larvae** hatch out with tiny **gills**. In a few months, the young newts have grown lungs and nostrils. Soon they are crawling through forests, soaked by autumn rain.

Protective mother

The female mudpuppy is unusual as she stays near her eggs to protect them for about 6 weeks. When they hatch, the little mudpuppies stay close to the nesting site and their mother. They are about 2.5 centimetres long with colourful bodies. Already they have small front and back legs.

▼ This is a common frog tadpole before metamorphosis.

► Very few of the tadpoles forming this **frogspawn** will grow to be adults.

algae   types of simple plant without stems that grow in water or wet places
metamorphosis   change from being a larva to being an adult

Frog life cycle

A new **tadpole** has a mouth, tail and **gills**. A few days after it has hatched, it can swim and feed on **algae**. After 4 weeks, skin grows over its gills. Then come tiny teeth, which help it grind up solid food. By 2 months, tiny legs sprout and the body grows longer. It now starts to eat dead insects and some plants. The front legs begin to bulge and pop out at the elbow. Now with a proper head, the tadpole looks like a tiny frog with a tail. By 12 weeks, the tail is a stub and the tadpole is a real little frog! Soon this froglet leaves the water and begins a new life on land. Next spring it will return to **spawn** and the whole cycle starts again.

Slow development

Some frogs that live high up in the mountains or in other colder places might take a whole winter to go through the tadpole stage. The cold slows everything down. Where it is cool, they take it easy.

◄ This froglet has nearly completed its change from a tadpole.

spawn   lay eggs and produce young

Daddy long legs

A midwife is a nurse who helps in the birth of babies and looking after them. Midwife toads also have a clever way of looking after their young. The male wraps the string of eggs round his back legs. They stay there until they hatch out. Then the male pops the tadpoles into water and off they swim.

Parents and young

Although amphibians are not often caring parents, a few frogs take the job seriously.

As there were not any ponds in the Australian desert for the gastric brooding frog to lay its eggs, it swallowed them. It kept the eggs in its stomach. The baby frogs would then hop from the mother's mouth when they were past the **tadpole** stage. It is amazing that the juices inside the mother's stomach did not harm the young frogs. Sadly, these frogs are now **extinct**.

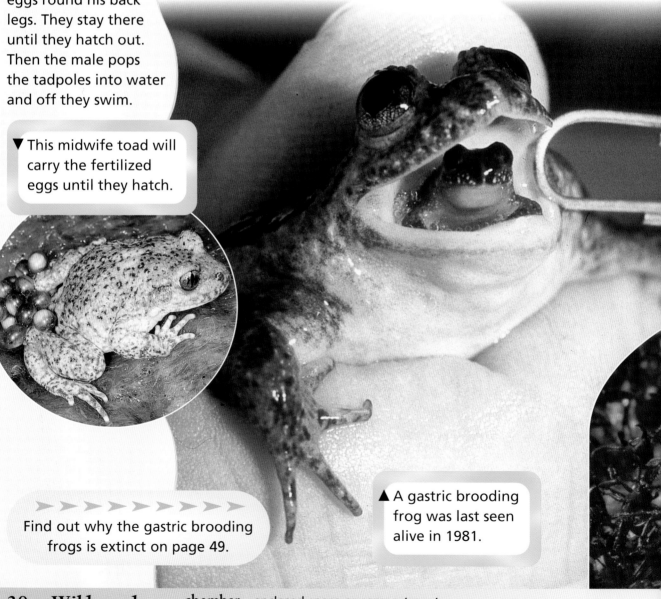

▼ This midwife toad will carry the fertilized eggs until they hatch.

Find out why the gastric brooding frogs is extinct on page 49.

▲ A gastric brooding frog was last seen alive in 1981.

chamber enclosed space or compartment
extinct died out, never to return

Backpack

Surinam toads live in South America. After they have mated, the male presses the eggs onto the female's back. Within hours her skin grows around them. Eighty days later, the eggs hatch and the young pop out of the mother's back.

Mother frogs

Strawberry poison dart frogs do not lay eggs in water but on land. Just as the tadpoles are about to hatch, the mother carries them on her back to a tree. Here, she finds small, water-filled leaves. The tadpoles develop in these tiny but safe pools and the mother feeds them with her spare eggs. When they are ready, the froglets hop off to find their own food.

Father frogs

The Darwin's frog lives in South American streams. The female lays about 30 eggs and the male guards them for about 2 weeks. Then he picks them up and pops them in his **vocal pouch**. The tadpoles grow in his baggy chin skin, feeding off their own egg **yolk**. When they are tiny frogs about 1 centimetre long, they hop out and swim off.

Foster parents

Recently scientists found some tadpoles in ant nests! The ants fed the tadpoles in little watery **chambers** under the nest. Is this some sort of baby-sitting service for baby frogs? We still do not know what goes on in these South American nests.

▼ South American ant nests like this one may hold a nursery for tadpoles.

vocal pouch   'skin bag' or dewlap at the throat
yolk   thick part inside an egg, such as the yellow part of a hen's egg

31

Defence

It is not easy being an amphibian, as many **predators** want to eat you. Snakes, birds, fish, **mammals** and other amphibians see you as a tasty snack.

Poison in frogs

The tiny poison-arrow frogs of South American rainforests fight back. They make the most **lethal venom** of all amphibians. There are 170 **species** of these brightly coloured frogs, and about 3 species are deadly. A tiny drop of their poison can kill a human. Yet poison-arrow frogs lose their poison if they do not eat their natural diet of rainforest insects.

The Amazon Indians use the frogs' venom on the tips of their arrows. They hunt by shooting the arrows into animals, which quickly die. Scraping a dart across a frog's back will give enough poison to kill many wild animals.

Keep off!

Frogs and toads often respond to threats by puffing up their bodies so they appear much larger than their real size. Others, like the poison-arrow frog below, have bright colours to warn off attackers. Warning spots say one thing – 'I might be poisonous. Eat me if you dare!'

cancer   disease in which some cells in some parts of the body change or grow out of control

▼ Piaroa Indians in Venezuela make good use of frog poison.

Useful poison

The chemicals found in a golden poison-arrow frog (shown below) may one day be used in human medicine. The effects they have on the heart can be put to good use for some patients with heart problems. Other frogs are being used to help doctors develop painkillers. A new drug, known as ABT-594, may be able to help ease the pain of some **cancers**.

SMUGGLING KILLER FROGS WARNING

People who collect frogs are at risk. Poison-arrow frogs are being smuggled round the world to meet the demand for colourful pets. Anyone who handles one of these South American frogs could be dead in seconds. If the poison gets into a cut, the **victim** will die from an instant heart attack.

A man who was stopped at Heathrow Airport, London in 1999 had 15 deadly frogs hidden in cans. They had enough poison to kill everyone on the plane with plenty to spare.

Even though these colourful frogs begin to lose much of their poison if they do not eat insects from the jungle, you must be on the alert. People who touch a poison-arrow frog must scrub their hands immediately.

lethal venom   deadly poison
victim   someone who gets hurt or killed

Rough-skinned newts

Rough-skinned newts like the one below are common in the USA, mainly along the West Coast, all the way north to Alaska. They are one of the most plentiful amphibians in western Washington State, along with Pacific tree frogs, red-legged frogs and long-toed salamanders. That is quite a mixture.

Poison in newts

How do you stop something eating you? Easy – kill it first! That is how many amphibians survive in their tough world. **Glands** in their skin make some of the strongest **venoms** we know.

The rough-skinned newt is sometimes called the orange-bellied newt and it is one of the most poisonous of all salamanders. Anything that bites it will spit it out instantly – apart from the common garter snake. This **reptile** is **immune** to the newt's poison. Any other **predator** would be dead in 10 minutes. Scientists have found that a single newt has enough poison to kill more than 1500 mice. They also tested 30 predators, from kingfishers and herons to bullfrogs and fish. In every case the newt killed them and it often crawled from their mouths within minutes of being swallowed whole.

antidote   medicine to make a poison safe
con   something false, a trick

Handle with care

A tiny drop of the venom of a rough-skinned newt is enough to kill an adult human. And there is no known **antidote** for its poison. This newt needs to be handled with care. In 1979 a 29-year-old man from Oregon, USA made a bet that he could safely eat one. He did not win the bet and died soon after swallowing the newt.

Two of a kind

Other North American newts are also poisonous. The colours of the Californian newt warns birds and snakes not to eat it. This works so well that its cousin the red salamander copies its trick. But it is just a **con**. The red salamander is not poisonous at all, but would make a tasty snack. How sneaky is that?

Rock and roll

The Mount Lyell salamander lives under rocks below cliffs in the Sierra Nevada Mountains in California. When its rock is lifted up, the salamander curls into a ball and rolls away down the hillside away from a predator.

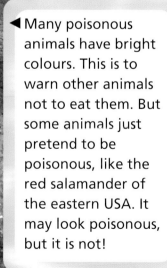

◀ Many poisonous animals have bright colours. This is to warn other animals not to eat them. But some animals just pretend to be poisonous, like the red salamander of the eastern USA. It may look poisonous, but it is not!

immune   protected against infection or poison

Secret weapon

A really big cane toad will squirt a jet of poison up to 1 metre away. If a predator still picks up the toad in its mouth, the poison will burn its lips so it will drop the toad quickly. It is just as well, because eating the toad would be a **fatal** mistake.

The deadly toad

A big toad can be a big problem. In the 1930s, beetles were harming sugar cane. So South American cane toads were let loose to eat the pests in Australia, the Caribbean and the USA. The cane toads did a good job and many grew to over 20 centimetres. But then they began to take over and threaten other animals. Anything that tried to eat one was killed in minutes. The cane toad's defence is just too good. Its poisonous skin is deadly.

When scientists first took the toads to the sugar cane fields, they did not realize the females could lay up to 35,000 eggs at a time, often twice a year. That is a lot of new toads!

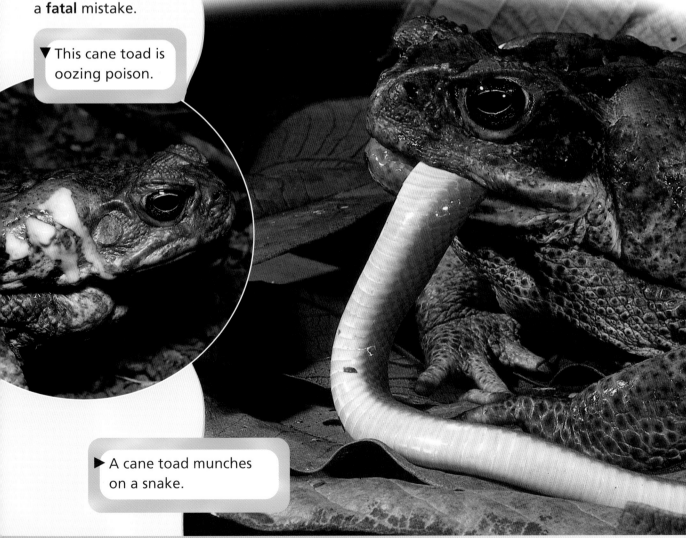

▼ This cane toad is oozing poison.

► A cane toad munches on a snake.

carrion　dead and rotting flesh
fatal　causing death

Giant toads with giant appetites

Once cane toads lived only from Texas to South America. Not any more. They were let loose in Florida, where they now kill dogs and cats that lick them. The toads eat anything they can swallow. Often they eat pet food left outside, **carrion** and household scraps. They gulp down insects such as beetles, ants, crickets and bugs. **Marine** snails, smaller toads and frogs, young snakes, and small **mammals** are also on the menu. Cane toads are a nuisance to bee-keepers as they eat many honeybees.

The cane toads' strong poison does not keep them totally safe. Some snakes can eat them and some birds will turn them over and eat only their non-poisonous insides. Even so, these **predators** have to handle the toads with care. One wrong gulp could be lethal.

Heavy brigade

The cane toad is sometimes called the giant cane toad because of its size. The male sits on Australian lawns and makes a high-pitched *brrr* call. In towns, groups of cane toads hang about street lamps eating insects drawn to the light. They are the thugs of the amphibian world.

▲ Cane toads get together for a meal.

marine   to do with the sea

Colour and camouflage

Looks are important if you are an amphibian. It could be a matter of life or death. A good **disguise** can fool a **predator**. Stripes are useful as they break up the body shape and make you look like something else.

Some amphibians can change colour. White's tree frogs are usually light green. When they move out of the sun into the shade, they often turn light brown.

One type of frog **survives** in the desert by changing colour from brown to white in bright sunlight. This reflects the sun and stops it getting sunburn or drying up.

Sometimes if danger is near it is best to look dead. Some frogs and toads simply lie on their backs and act like a **corpse**. Then predators will ignore them and not bother to attack.

▲ The burrowing frog is well camouflaged in the woodlands of Australia.

Combat dress

Many amphibians have a kind of combat uniform. Their **mottled** green and brown skin blends in with the undergrowth and makes them very hard to see. African clawed frogs can even change their colour to match their background. That makes perfect **camouflage**.

camouflage   colour that matches the background
corpse   dead body

Warning messages

Fire-bellied toads have black and orange spots on their backs. They blend in with the moss and plants in streams where they live. But if startled on land, they raise their head to show their bright orange belly. Such bright colours flash when the toads move and this startles a predator. The toads then have a few seconds to leap away.

The four-eyed frog of Chile in South America has a pair of spots on its rear. These are poison **glands** with spots on them. They look just like eyes from behind. When the frog feels any threat, it will show its fake eyespots and make them swell up. This should fool the predator and make it think twice about taking a bite.

Salamander tails

Salamanders whip their bright tails about to fend off predators. If that does not confuse them, they shake the whole tail off. The tail wriggles on the ground and **distracts** the attacker while the salamander slips away to grow a new tail.

◄ The fire-bellied toad in camouflage gear.

disguise   change of appearance to look different
mottled   spots and patches of colour

Weird and wonderful

Scientists have studied amphibians for a long time. But these animals still raise many questions, puzzles and a lot of mystery.

Extreme conditions

Although most amphibians need to live in damp places, some can still **survive** extreme temperatures.

Icy salamander

The Siberian salamander can cope with the cold. The Arctic wilderness freezes for months, with temperatures often down to below −50 °C. The salamander becomes frozen in the soil and ice. Once this starts to melt, the salamander warms up and becomes active again.

Frozen alive

Wood frogs and the spring peeper of North America have to survive very cold winters. They sit in the ice and snow, covered only by a few leaves. Then they freeze as the temperature drops to about −8 °C. Ice crystals form around these frogs but they make a type of **anti-freeze** in their liver. This stops their organs from freezing up completely, even though their heart and lungs 'close down'.

When the spring comes, the frogs thaw from the inside out. They wake up and their hearts begin to pump again as they defrost.

▼ Some salamanders can survive in the snowy mountains of Siberia.

40   Wild words

aboriginal   native
anti-freeze   liquid that does not freeze at temperatures below 0 °C

The long wait

Australian desert frogs have a hard time. It does not just get hot in the desert – it is also very dry. It may not rain for 10 years. So how does each frog survive? It goes under ground and wraps itself in the skin it has **shed**. Then it waits… and waits. Its **bladder** stores water, which keeps it alive for many years. **Aboriginal** Australians have even managed to track down these frogs to use as emergency water supplies in the desert.

When the first rain starts to wet the ground, the frogs sense that it is time to wake up. Suddenly the desert fills with croaking frogs hopping about in the cool rain and mud.

Would you believe it?

The African clawed toad and the yellow-bellied toad make their own medicine. They live in warm, **stagnant** water full of **viruses**. In the heat, their skin makes a chemical that fights viruses, keeps them healthy and makes them fighting fit.

▼ The Australian desert frog is sometimes called a water-holding frog.

▼ An African clawed toad is really a frog!

bladder sac in the body containing water or urine
virus very tiny living thing that causes some diseases

A toad in the hole

For years people have found toads in weird places. Way back in 1835, a man called John Bruton saw a slab of rock fall off a wagon near Coventry, England. It cracked open to show a hole in the middle. Out of that hole fell a live toad. Bruton could not believe it so he took the toad home to show everyone.

Unsolved mystery

For years there has been a big mystery about some amphibians. They seem to be able to **survive** inside solid rock. Builders have knocked down old walls only to find the odd toad sealed up inside. Or a rock may be cracked open and a frog sits and croaks in a hollow inside. Can this really happen?

In 1995 a boy at Rhyl High School in Wales, UK had a surprise. He picked up an empty soft drink can. At least, he thought it was empty. Inside there was a frog. But it was too big to get out. So how had it got in and how had it survived? Perhaps it hopped inside as a tiny frog and fed on insects. The damp would also help it to grow.

▲ Cane toads turn up in all sorts of places.

cavity   gap or a hole

Trapped

Maybe there are frogs and toads all over the world locked inside cans and stones right now! One idea is that tiny young amphibians hide in small cracks in rocks and openings in cans. They wriggle into tiny hollows deep inside. Here it is cool and damp – just right for a frog or toad to live and grow. Insects also go into these cracks to shelter. The amphibian snaps them up and grows too big to get out again. It becomes trapped. A toad could live for years like this with a supply of insects, some moisture and a bit of luck. This has not been proved but it seems the most likely **theory**.

Strange discovery

In 1982 some railway workers were cutting through rocks in Te Kuiti, New Zealand. In the middle of the rock they found two live frogs sealed in a **cavity**. How on earth did they get there? Mysteries like this have meant that frogs and toads have been linked to magic and witches for hundreds of years.

▼ These froglets are leaving the water, maybe to set up home in a can!

▲ Cracks in rocks give amphibians ideal hiding places.

theory   idea that attempts to explain how something happens

Hitching a ride

Dainty green tree frogs like the one below come from Queensland, Australia. They now appear all over the world. Their natural home is in banana trees, but they often ride on bananas that are sent 2400 kilometres (1500 miles) south. It is thought that up to 8000 frogs end up in the southern port of Melbourne each year. Then ships take them overseas!

Travelling frogs

One of nature's surprises is that some amphibians spend their lives not in water but in the treetops. But that is not all. From India to Sumatra in South-east Asia, it seems that some frogs can fly!

There may be 800 **species** of tree frog of all colours. There must still be species in the rainforests we do not yet know about. Scientists are still finding out some of their secrets. Many of these frogs never come down from the trees. They even mate and lay their eggs high in the branches. When the **tadpoles** hatch out they fall down into the plants and puddles below and only climb back up again when they have got their sticky feet. A few have even stranger feet. Their feet become like wings.

► The Wallace's tree frog has suction pads on its fingers and toes and can stick to upright surfaces when it lands.

glide   float through the air rather than using power to fly
import   bring into the country from abroad

Flying frogs

Flying frogs have four big feet. These are parachute-like flaps, which act as air-brakes when the frogs **glide** from tree to tree or leaf to leaf. These frogs are really gliders rather than fliers. Without these special flaps, they would just fall.

The webs on the toes of Wallace's tree frog are no longer used for swimming. They allow the frog to glide as far as 15 metres through the air, although it will lose a lot of height. Even so, this is a great way of travelling through the trees to find food or to escape from a hungry snake. It is the closest an amphibian gets to being a bird.

On the move

Hawaii's Big Island is being overrun by tree frogs. Numbers of **non-native** Caribbean frogs have soared in just 2 years in Hawaii. They have arrived on **imported** plants. Every night, the frogs eat tens of thousands of insects, which would otherwise be eaten by local birds. People say they cannot sleep because of these noisy frogs.

► Trinidad leaf frogs can hide themselves in plants that get moved around.

---

non-native   not a local species

Frog language

Frogs often squeak when they are hurt or frightened. But their normal call is lower and more like a croak. Each country has a different way to describe a frog's call:

Russian	kva-kva
Afrikaans (South Africa)	kwaak-kwaak
Hebrew	kwa kwa
Japanese	kerokero
Turkish	vrak vrak

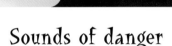

▶ Fringe-lipped bats from South America are frog-eating predators.

Sounds of danger

Amphibians are not always the silent animals they appear to be. Sounds are important in their dangerous world.

Some frogs are their own worst enemy. When they croak, it is a signal to a frog-eating bat called a fringe-lipped bat. The bat picks up the sound waves and soon knows there is supper about.

A pond could be full of croaking frogs but as soon as a bat appears, all the frogs fall silent. None moves. They know any sound will bring the bat swooping down, ready to strike. One move and the bat will sense where a frog is and will catch it. Survival for the frogs means knowing when to be quiet until the danger has passed.

cocoon   silky case for protection
drought   long period with no rain and a shortage of water

Siren sounds

A big danger facing amphibians is **drought**. Sirens are a type of salamander with short front legs and none at the back. Sirens live in water but have to burrow deep into mud when ponds dry up.

To escape death, each siren wraps itself in a **cocoon** of slime and old skin. This covers its body to stop it drying up. The body then slows right down. The siren stays very still and may live like this for more than a year. When it rains, the ponds fill with water again and the siren comes to life.

Predators try to catch sirens as they emerge. When they are grasped, sirens make a yelping sound. Some are even said to bark.

Toad calls

Natterjack toads are found in south-west and central Europe, but are rare in the UK.

Natterjacks are thought to be Europe's noisiest amphibian. The male's call can be heard for several kilometres. It is a loud **rasping** call, which sounds like *rrrrRup, rrrrRup*.

◄ This natterjack toad is showing how he makes his very loud croak.

rasping   grating sound or a hoarse noise from the throat

Amphibians in danger

A number of amphibians are now very rare. Some might soon disappear forever. Much work is going on to save some of these **endangered species**.

Under threat

The corroboree frog lives only in the Snowy Mountains of Australia. But in the last few years nearly 70 per cent of these bright yellow-and-black amphibians have disappeared. No one really knows why. It could be because humans and their animals trample the land where the frogs live. But it might be a **fungus** that is killing them. Plans are under way to help save this species.

The golden alpine salamander is now very seriously endangered. Water has been drained in Italy where it lives so its **habitat** is under threat. People have also caught these salamanders to keep as pets.

Missing toad

The golden toad (shown above) has not been seen in Central America since 1989 when people thought only about eleven were left. This toad is now believed to be **extinct** because of **global warming**. Males were a brilliant orange colour but females were dark and **mottled** with yellow-edged red blobs.

> ▶ Selling or trading palmate newts like this one is illegal.

DDT   chemical used to control insect pests
global warning   warming up of the Earth due to burning fossil fuels

Disappearing frogs

Mississippi gopher frogs once lived in large numbers in the south-east of the USA. But hardly any have been seen in the state of Louisiana since 1962. Only one breeding group is now known to live in the Mississippi region. Scientists think the frogs have **declined** because their habitat has been spoiled.

Disappearing newts

Some of the European newts are now rare and endangered in many countries. The southern crested newt is probably the fastest disappearing of all. The most likely reasons for this are:

* the treatment of water with **DDT** in the 1950s in the battle against **malaria**
* the introduction of trout, which compete for food
* the lower water levels due to the high demand for water from tourists and farmers
* the catching of newts to sell as pets.

Changing fortunes

The gastric brooding frog (shown below) was first discovered in 1973, but it had vanished from the wild 10 years later. So what made this rare frog become extinct? Perhaps the drier **climate** or water **pollution** may have wiped it out. Some scientists think a **virus** may have killed many of the frogs.

malaria   deadly disease spread by mosquitoes
pollution   spoiling natural things with dangerous chemicals, fumes or rubbish

Poisoned water

Chemicals used to kill pests may be changing the sex of leopard frogs in the USA. Leopard frogs like the one below are the most common species of frog found naturally in North America. They are very sensitive to changes in the water because they **absorb** it through their skin. **Pesticides** could be affecting the frogs' ability to mate.

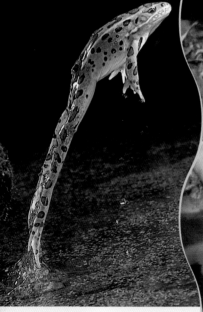

Amphibians and us

Amphibians have always **fascinated** us. It is not just their amazing 'double life' and how they emerge from water. Their colours, noises and poisons have amazed people through the ages. In fact, toads, newts and frogs were thought to have magical powers and were used in witches' spells. People believed that harming a frog would bring floods.

Amphibians have **survived** for up to 400 million years. Despite massive changes that wiped out the dinosaurs, amphibians are still with us. Yet scientists are worried. One recent study showed amphibians have been disappearing for the past 40 years. Their numbers go down by about 4 per cent each year. We are not always certain why this is. It is probably because amphibians soak in water and air through their sensitive skins. They soon show signs of **environmental** damage.

acid rain   rain high in acid from falling through smoke and poisoned air

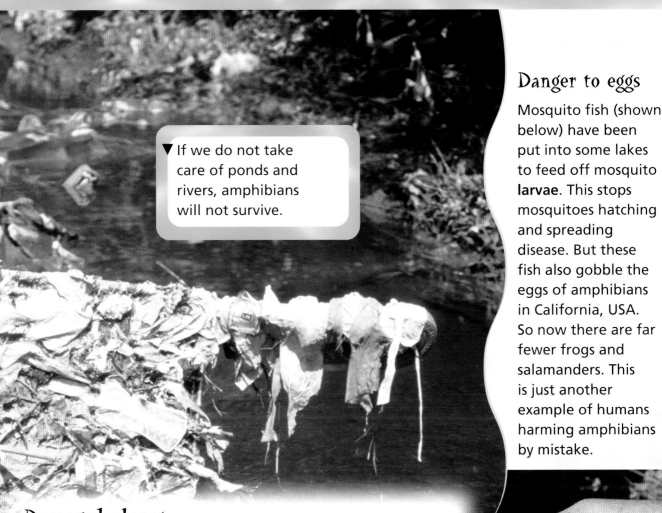

▼ If we do not take care of ponds and rivers, amphibians will not survive.

Danger to eggs

Mosquito fish (shown below) have been put into some lakes to feed off mosquito **larvae**. This stops mosquitoes hatching and spreading disease. But these fish also gobble the eggs of amphibians in California, USA. So now there are far fewer frogs and salamanders. This is just another example of humans harming amphibians by mistake.

Damaged planet

If you see a healthy frog in the wild, it is a sign of a healthy environment. **Pollution** caused by people is one of their biggest threats. **Acid rain** is just one threat to their ponds. American scientists think **climate** change may also be putting amphibians under threat.

Twenty **species** of amphibian have probably become **extinct** in the last 10 years. **Global warming** and the drying out of **spawning** sites may be only one reason. Disease and **fungi** attack amphibians in their warm, damp homes. In fact, scientists have treated some frog diseases with the same creams we use to cure athlete's foot in humans.

We still have much to learn about these amazing animals that have shared our planet for so long.

environmental   to do with our surroundings and habitats
pesticide   poison sprayed on the land to kill unwanted insects

51

Find out more

Websites

BBC Nature
The 'Wildfacts' website is packed with photos and information about all sorts of animals.
bbc.co.uk/nature

Enchanted Learning
The 'Animal Printout' page has pictures, activities and information on lots of different amphibians.
enchantedlearning .com

UK Safari
Website with information and photos of UK frogs, newts and toads.
uksafari.com

Books
Animal Kingdom: Amphibians, Sally Morgan (Raintree, 2004)
Keeping Unusual Pets: Lizards, Peter Heathcote (Heineman Library, 2004)
Keeping Unusual Pets: Salamanders, Peter Heathcote (Heineman Library, 2004)

World Wide Web
If you want to find out more about amphibians, you can search the internet using keywords like these:
* 'Chinese giant salamanders'
* common + frog
* horned toad

You can also find your own keywords by using headings or words from this book. Use the following search tips to help you find the most useful websites.

Search tips

There are billions of pages on the Internet so it can be difficult to find exactly what you are looking for.

For example, if you just type in 'water' on a search engine like Google, you will get a list of 50 million web pages. These search skills will help you find useful websites more quickly:

- Use simple keywords instead of whole sentences
- Use two to six keywords in a search, putting the most important words first
- Be precise – only use names of people, places or things
- If you want to find words that go together, put quote marks around them
- Use the advanced section of your search engine
- Use the + sign between keywords to link them. For example, typing + KS3 after your keyword will help you find web pages at the right level.

Where to search

Search engine

A search engine looks through a small proportion of the web and lists all sites that match the words in the search box. It can give thousands of links, but the best matches are at the top of the list, on the first page.
Try bbc.co.uk/search

Search directory

A search directory is like a library of websites that have been sorted by a person instead of a computer. You can search by keyword or subject and browse through the different sites like you look through books on a library shelf.
A good example is yahooligans.com

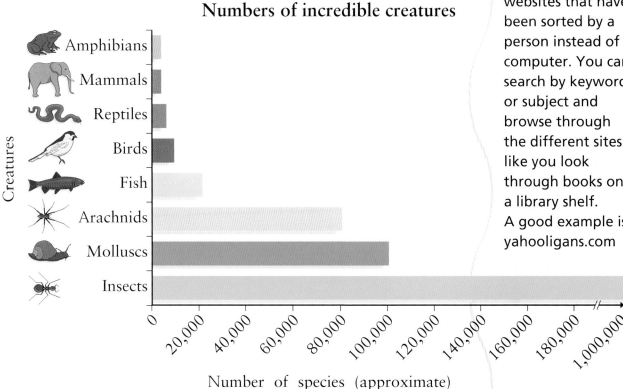

Numbers of incredible creatures

Creatures: Amphibians, Mammals, Reptiles, Birds, Fish, Arachnids, Molluscs, Insects

Number of species (approximate)

0, 20,000, 40,000, 60,000, 80,000, 100,000, 120,000, 140,000, 160,000, 180,000, 1,000,000

Glossary

aboriginal native

absorb take in something or soak it up

acid rain rain high in acid from falling through smoke and poisoned air

algae types of simple plant without stems that grow in water or wet places

ancient from a past age long ago

antidote medicine to make a poison safe

anti-freeze liquid that does not freeze at temperatures below 0 °C

battering ram heavy rod used to knock down walls and doors

bladder sac in the body containing water or urine

caecilian ('see-silly-un') burrowing amphibian that has no limbs

camouflage colour that matches the background

cancer disease in which some cells in some parts of the body change or grow out of control

captivity a cage or tank – as in a zoo

carbon dioxide gas that animals breathe out

carnivore meat-eater

carrion dead and rotting flesh

cavity gap or a hole

chamber enclosed space or compartment

climate general weather conditions in an area over a period of time

cocoon silky case for protection

communicate make contact and understand another's signals

con something false, a trick

corpse dead body

cyanide a deadly poison

DDT chemical used to control insect pests

decline lose strength or fall in numbers

dew water droplets that form on plants during cool nights

dewlap loose flap of skin at the throat

disguise change of appearance to look different

distract draw away the attention

drought long period with no rain and a shortage of water

embryo tiny group of growing cells formed from a fertilized egg

endangered at risk of disappearing forever

environmental to do with surroundings and habitats

evolve develop and change over time

extinct died out, never to return

fascinate capture the interest

fatal causing death

fertilize when a sperm joins an egg to form a new individual

fossil very old remains of things that once lived, found in mud and rock

frogspawn jelly-like mass of fertilized frog eggs

fungus (plural: **fungi**) type of mould that grows in damp places

gills flaps that some animals have to breathe under water

gland part of the body that makes hormones and other substances

glide float through the air rather than using power to fly

global warming warming up of the Earth due to burning fossil fuels such as coal and oil

habitat natural home of an animal or plant

hibernate 'close down' the body and rest when it is too cold or dry

immune protected against infection or poison

import bring into the country from abroad

invertebrate animal without a backbone

larva (plural: **larvae**) young of an animal that is very different from the adult

leaf litter damp, decaying leaves that litter the ground in forests

lethal venom deadly poison

limb moving part that sticks out from a body like an arm and a leg

malaria deadly disease spread by mosquitoes

mammal warm-blooded animal that has hair and feeds its young on milk

marine to do with the sea

metamorphosis change from being a larva to being an adult

mottled spots and patches of colour

muscular having strong muscles

nerves fibres that carry messages between the brain and other parts of the body

non-native not a local species

nourishment food that supplies important nutrients to the body

nutrients important substances found in food and needed by the body

oxygen one of the gases in air and water that all living things need

pelvis area of bone between the hips

pesticide poison sprayed on to crops to kill insects and pests

pollution spoiling natural things with dangerous chemicals, fumes or rubbish

predator animal that hunts and eats other animals

prey animal that is killed and eaten by other animals

propel drive along and push forward

rasping grating sound or a hoarse noise from the throat

reptile cold-blooded animal with scales, such as a snake or lizard

scales small bony plates that protect the skin – as on fish and reptiles

shed get rid of or lose

spawn lay eggs and produce young

species type of animal or plant

sperm male sex cell

spiny having lots of spines or spikes

stagnant still and lifeless

stalk hunt down by following and creeping up on a victim

survive stay alive despite danger and difficulties

swarm large group or mass of animals moving together

tadpole the young stage, or larva, of a frog or a toad

thaw when ice or snow melt

theory idea that attempts to explain how something happens

toxic poisonous

venom poison

vertebrate animal with a backbone

vibration quivering movement or fast trembling

victim someone who gets hurt or killed

virus very tiny living thing that causes some diseases

vocal pouch 'skin bag' or dewlap at the throat

whirlwind column of air whirling round and round very fast

yolk thick part inside an egg, such as the yellow part of a hen's egg

Index

Series in the *Freestyle Curriculum Strand* include:

Turbulent Planet

Energy Essentials

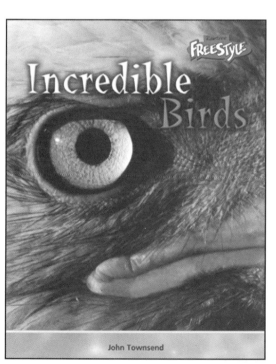

Incredible Creatures

Material Matters

Find out about the other titles in these series on our website www.raintreepublishers.co.uk